Reduce, Reuse, Recycle

Food

Alexandra Fix

www.heinemann.co.uk/library

Visit our website to find out more information about **Heinemann Library** books.

To order:

☎ Phone ++44 (0)1865 888066

▤ Send a fax to ++44 (0)1865 314091

▢ Visit the Heinemann Bookshop at www.heinemann.co.uk/library to browse our catalogue and order online.

First published in Great Britain by Heinemann Library, Halley Court, Jordan Hill, Oxford OX2 8EJ, part of Harcourt Education.
Heinemann is a registered trademark of Harcourt Education Ltd.

Editorial: Cassie Mayer and Diyan Leake
Design: Steven Mead and Debbie Oatley
Picture research: Ruth Blair
Production: Duncan Gilbert

Origination: Chroma Graphics (Overseas) Pte Ltd
Printed and bound in China by South China Printing Company Ltd

ISBN 978 0 431 90754 3

12 11 10 09 08
10 9 8 7 6 5 4 3 2 1

British Library Cataloguing in Publication Data
Fix, Alexandra, 1950-
Food. - (Reduce, reuse, recycle)
1. Organic wastes - Juvenile literature 2. Organic wastes - Recycling - Juvenile literature 3. Food industry and trade - Waste disposal - Juvenile literature 4. Food industry and trade - Waste minimization - Juvenile literature
I. Title
363.7'288

Acknowledgements
The publishers would like to thank the following for permission to reproduce photographs: Alamy pp. **16** (Charles Stirling), **23** (Jim West), **27** (Graham Corney); Ardea pp. **7** (Jean Michel Labat), **8** (M. Watson), **18** (Chris Knights), **19** (John Cancalosi), **22** (John Daniels); Corbis pp. **4** (Paul Thompson), **5** (Patrick Glardino), **10** (Steve Miller/Eye Ubiquitous), **11** (Chuck Savage), **12** (Theo Allofs/Zefa), **20** (Charles Gullung/Zefa), **25** (Royalty Free), **26** (Mika/Zefa); FLPA pp. **15** (Jim Brandenburg/Minden Pictures), **28** (Mike J. Thomas); Naturepl.com p. **9** (Lynn M. Stone), Photolibrary.com pp. **6**, **13**, **14** (Jon Arnold Images), **17**, **21** (Workbook, Inc.), **24** (Botanica).

Cover photograph reproduced with permission of Corbis (Lois Ellen Frank).

The publishers would like to thank Simon Miller for his assistance in the preparation of this book.

Every effort has been made to contact copyright holders of any material reproduced in this book. Any omissions will be rectified in subsequent printings if notice is given to the publishers.

Contents

Some words are shown in bold, **like this**. You can find out what they mean by looking in the glossary.

What is food waste?

Food is wasted every day. Leftover food at restaurants is thrown away with the rubbish. In homes and shops, spoiled or out-of-date food often gets thrown away.

Food waste often ends up in the bin.

↑ Taking more than you can eat creates food waste.

Food waste is food that is thrown away.
Much of the food that is grown in the world
goes to waste. If we buy and eat food more
wisely we can reduce food waste.

Why do we need food?

Food has **nutrients** that help the body grow. Vegetables such as broccoli, carrots, and spinach have vitamins and minerals that keep the body healthy. Fruit, beans, nuts, grains, and dairy products are also important to a healthy diet.

A healthy diet includes lots of vegetables, fruit, and grains.

Being active is an important part of staying healthy.

Food gives the body **energy** to move.
The body uses food as **fuel** so it can play
sport and do other activities. The brain
needs food to stay active, too.

Where does food come from?

Most food is grown at large farms. Farmers grow crops such as vegetables, fruit, and grains. Some people grow food in their own garden.

This lettuce is ready to be picked for salads.

These dairy cows give us fresh milk.

Some farmers raise animals for meat and dairy products. Some fish are raised in special ponds called fish farms. Most fish are caught in seas and rivers.

How does food get to our homes?

These cans of food are filled by a machine at a food processing plant.

After food crops are **harvested**, some food is taken to local farm shops or supermarkets. Many crops are shipped long distances to be sold in other countries.

Some of the crops go to a **food processing plant**. They are prepared and packaged. Food might be frozen or sealed in metal cans, glass jars, or plastic containers.

Many processed foods are sold at supermarkets.

How can we buy food more wisely?

Lorries and ships need diesel to move food from place to place. Diesel is made from oil, a **non-renewable resource**. Once we use up the earth's oil supply it will be gone forever.

↑ Food may be taken far from where it was grown.

Whenever you can, buy food grown near your **community**.

Buying food from local farmers wastes fewer non-renewable resources. The food is moved only a short distance. This uses less diesel.

Will we always have food?

Food is a **renewable resource**. We can grow more food as we use it. In many places of the world, enough food is grown to feed everyone.

These fields of wheat are ready to be **harvested**.

Poor soil and bad weather make it difficult to grow food in some areas.

Some countries cannot grow the food they need. They may not be able to pay for food to be **imported** into their country. In some places, there are people who do not have enough money to buy food.

When we waste food, more food has to be grown. It takes **fuel** to grow, process, and transport food. Most of the fuel for this work comes from oil: a **non-renewable resource**.

Large farm machines use fuel made from oil.

Rubbish lorries dump waste at landfill sites.

Fuel is also used to take food waste to **landfill sites**. The rubbish lorry runs on diesel made from oil. If we reduce food waste, we will waste less fuel.

How can we reduce food waste?

You can reduce food waste at home or school. Take only the food you can eat. Then eat what you have taken.

Keep leftovers in containers that can be washed and reused.

Put leftovers in the fridge right away so they do not go off. If you cannot finish a restaurant meal, take your leftovers home if you can.

Use leftover breadcrumbs to feed the birds in your garden.

You can reduce food waste by using all the food you cook. Leftover chicken can be used in a soup. Water used to cook vegetables can also be added to soups.

Restaurants and supermarkets often give extra food to shelters. These are places that collect food for people who need it. You can take food to shelters, too.

Many **community** groups collect dried goods for those in need.

How can we recycle food waste?

Leftover food that cannot be used again can be **recycled**. It is broken down and changed into **compost**. Compost is made from food scraps and plant waste.

Compost adds **nutrients** to soil that help plants to grow.

Compost eventually turns into a brown, rich soil.

The scraps and waste are mixed together in a heap that is usually kept outside. Over time, these break down and create a natural **fertilizer**. Fertilizer is mixed with soil to help plants grow.

How can you take action?

You can help reduce food waste. Ask family and friends to be more careful about wasting food. Use leftovers to make a new meal.

Only take as much food as you can eat.

You can add food scraps to a
compost container every day.

At home, ask your family to start a **compost** heap to **recycle** food waste. Help collect kitchen scraps and garden waste to add to the compost heap. If we reduce our food waste, we can help keep our planet clean.

Make a compost heap

Ask an adult to help you with this project.

You can begin a simple **compost** heap.

1. Make a small heap of dried leaves and add soil. Add equal amounts of green and brown materials (see page 29).

2. Turn the heap with a spade or garden fork at least once a week.
3. Add a little water if the heap gets too dry.

After several months, the mixture will begin to break down into a dark, rich compost that can be added to your garden.

Green (or wet) materials include:
grass cuttings, old flowers, weeds, and kitchen scraps such as eggshells, vegetable or fruit peelings, coffee grounds, and tea bags.

Brown (or dry) materials include:
dead leaves, straw, wood chips, old potting soil, and shredded newspaper.

Glossary

community   group of people who live in one area

compost   food scraps and plant waste that can
be added to soil

energy   power to do work

environment   natural surroundings for people, animals, and plants

fertilizer   substance added to soil to help plants grow

**food processing
    plant**   place where food is prepared, canned,
and packaged

fuel   something that is burned for power or heat

harvest   picking crops when they are ready to eat

import   bring goods into one country from another
country

landfill site   large area where rubbish is dumped, crushed,
and covered with soil

**non-renewable
    resource**   material taken from the earth that cannot be
replaced by nature

nutrient   substance in food that keeps the body healthy
and helps it grow

pollute   harm the air, soil, or water with chemicals or waste

recycle   break down a material and use it again to make
a new product

renewable resource something that can be replaced by nature

Find out more

Books to read
Food: Bananas, Louise Spilsbury (Heinemann Library, 2003)

Where Does Rubbish Go? Sophy Tahta (Usborne Publishing Ltd, 2001)

Why Should I Recycle? Jen Green (Hodder Wayland, 2002).

Websites
Waste Watch work to teach people about reducing, reusing, and recycling waste. You can visit www.recyclezone.org.uk to find out more information about waste and to try some online activities..

Find out where you can recycle in your local area at: www.recyclenow.com by typing in your postcode. You can also find out more about which items can be recycled, more facts about waste, and what you can do to help!

Index